THE
SALESMAN

"THE BEST THING THAT COULD HAPPENED TO ME"

LUIS G. MORENO CINTRÓN

THE SALESMAN

THE SALESMAN
"THE BEST THING THAT COULD HAPPENED
TO ME"

EDITOR:
MARÍA DEL PILAR MARÍN QUILES

DESIGN AND COVER:
ASTRID J. SEPÚLVEDA RODRÍGUEZ

TRANSLATOR:
ARIANE VELÁZQUEZ

PRODUCED IN PUERTO RICO
ISBN: 978-0-578-70722-8

DEDICATION

To all the men and women who go out each day to work to be able to have and offer the best quality of life to their families. Bless you and your families for your contributions.

CONTENTS

ACKNOWLEDGMENTS

A few years were needed for me to sit down and
write this book. I want to express my gratitude to
the people whose dedication and enthusiasm
made the publishing of it possible.

Pedro Hernandez Guilbe, Esq., for his immense
positivism and support from the start.

Mariel, my loving wife and partner who was in
charge of drafting and revisions of the Spanish
version, and for her continued motivation.

Marta and Mayela, for their love, kindness, and
strong faith, who have been a source of
inspiration. I love both of you and I am honored
that you are my sisters. And to the authors
of the thoughts whose wisdom has made
a significant mark in my life.

AUTHOR'S NOTE

It is a curious thing to look back at what you have lived and see the certain steps that took you to where you are at the moment, for example, what inspired me to write this book.

The idea of writing had been lurking in my head for a long time, and it was not until recently with the experience of managing a team of sales oriented people, that it detonated the necessary spark to starting to write this book. Certainly, it was an intriguing though, I would ask myself, why so many people want to work in the hard sales career without even thinking about the success? Even when we are all salespeople, being able to follow this career, or becoming a successful professional in the sales field will require at least two factors to be present. These factors are, having the need and a positive attitude. When I mention need is because the level of need we have as individuals is going to be directly related to the level of individual goals we have or we set for ourselves. We all have seen people who have very few materials things and live without any need because their goal level is low or even zero. We could then say that without goals there are no needs. We could then say that without goals there are no needs. Wanting to have material things will give us the need to work for them and while we are covering those needs we will transform our personality. The other factor is the positive attitude, which plays an important role in our development. If we achieve living with this positive energy, not only it will benefit ourselves, but we can also influence the people around us, we can spread our positive way of going through life.

To be able to become a sales professional is necessary to teach ourselves, following the teaching-learning process without the help of a teacher, basing it on the knowledge acquired through experience and our own critical judgement. This turns us into "autodidacts." As it is common knowledge, colleges and universities do not prepare persons to be professional salesmen or saleswomen, it is a nonexistent degree. That is one of the reasons that motivated me to write this book with the objective that it could be used as a tool to create or help professional sales people. After all, a sales professional is not born; it is made, just like a doctor, a lawyer or an accountant.

It is necessary to self-teach ourselves, same as the business man or woman who wants to have success needs to learn how to sell his or her ideas to others. Selling is synonym of communicate, show interest, listen, problem solve and to be ready to serve others daily. It does not matter which business you choose, the ability to communicate and sell is essential to have success.

In more than one occasion I challenged groups of salespeople with questions like: Why is that the sales leader in the office, Angel, has achieved what the rest of you have not? He made five times the medium income of his teammates. Is he five times smarter? No. Did he work five times harder than all of you? The answer is no. In fact, he was out of the job for health reasons for a considerable amount of time.

Does he have a better education? No. The difference Between Angel and the majority of the group is that Angel thinks five times bigger. Tests and studies show that success is determined not by the brain volume in each one, but by the volume of individual thoughts. Cases after cases in history show that the volume of bank accounts, happiness and general satisfaction depend on one's own thoughts. That is the magic. If thinking big, thinking about success, brings good things, why not everybody thinks in that way?

I think the answer is here. We are, more than we recognize, all a product of the thoughts that surround us and many of those thoughts are small, not big. Everything around you is part of an environment that tries to tie you down to a second class street;

towards what others think is their paradise. How

many times have we heard the phrase: "it's destiny,"

and in other occasions we hear "I'd have to be

born again to achieve it," and also "there are many

chiefs but few Indians" and then settling for

being an Indian. This same environment tells

us that there is a lot of competition. But, is it

really? If we convince ourselves that less people

think big then we have to conclude that there will

be less competition for people in the first class street.

 The simple judgements we offer here are not only

theory without proof, they are not conjectures or the

opinion of just one person; they are the product of a

proven approach to life situations. That you are

reading these pages demonstrates you are

widely interested in success and that you want to

achieve your wishes. You want to enjoy a magnificent lifestyle. You need to obtain all the good things you deserve. Being interested in success is a marvelous quality.

You have another admirable quality. The fact that you have this book in your hands reveals that you possess the intelligence to see which ones are the tools that will help you go where you desire to go. To build anything you need tools to achieve it. Many people in their intent of creating a better life forget that it has the useful tools that can help. You must not forget it.

You have, consequently, the two basic qualities necessary to extract a real advantage from this reading: the desire for bigger success and the

intelligence to select the tool that will help you
to realize that wish.

Think about success and you will live it, success
in income, in friendship and in respect. Start now:

*"What you get by achieving your goals is not as
important as what you become by achieving your
goals."*

Zig Ziglar

CHOOSE TO BE HAPPY

"Folks are usually about as happy as they make

their minds up to be."

Abraham Lincoln

My main purpose in writing this book is to offer

an important tool to help you accommodate your

thoughts in a way that you choose to be happy every

day. Whichever the challenge you may

encounter, whatever the circumstances that may

have you close to bring you down, you can choose

your answer. The way you live your life is yours

entirely. It does not depend on your circumstances;
it depends on your choosing to.

  A simple example of this is Thursdays in the
university culture. Thursday evening is the time
to meet up with friends to have a good time,
they choose that day. On the other hand, those
who belong to the labor forces have "social Fridays"
to celebrate, they choose that day to be the
happiest of the week, is just their pick. When you
wake up any day of the week bring up your
first thought to be 'Thank you God, I know this day
will be great!' Of course, we know some days are
harder than others, but if you program your mind
in a positive way you will not have to drag
your feet unmotivated, waiting for it to be
Friday to finally enjoy life and be happy. Your

attitude ought to be: "I'm alive and have many reasons to be alive in this moment." It is your choice to be happy, set out to enjoy this day and to have a blessed, prosperous and victorious year. You may encounter some setbacks, and your circumstances may change, but do not allow that to change your mind, keep it fixed on happiness.

We must understand that each day is a gift from God. When this day is over we will never get it back. If we make the mistake of being negative, discouraged, or grumpy, we would have wasted the day. Some persons waste away year after year being unhappy because somebody does not treat them correctly, or because they do not get what they want, or because their plans are not becoming reality as quickly as they want. The correct attitude is to make the decision of not wasting one more day. Celebrate each day like a gift from God.

  If you want to be happy you have to be happy with a purpose. When you wake up in the morning you cannot just sit and wait to see what kind of day you will have. You have to choose what kind of day you'll have. Things can happen every day that are not of our liking but we have to go on with the thought that that type of event belongs to the 10% of non-positive things we have no control over, but we still have the 90% of things we do have control over and they are there for good. A daily example of this: I have been in the parking lot waiting for a person to put their groceries in their car, buckle their kid in the car seat before leaving, and then seeing

another car coming from the opposite direction
and taking up the space I was waiting for. This may
make anyone very angry. But guess what? When one
has decided to be happy one cannot allow that the
things that are out of our control, those10%
of things, to ruin your well-being and happiness
when we still have 90% of things we can control
for our own good. So, smile and keep going,
better things will surely come. Keep your life
in the correct perspective; each and every one of
use has something in this moment to be happy
for: our health, our job, our family, or an opportunity.

You are not a victim, you are a winner. You would
not have obstacles and opposition if there were not
something wonderful in your goal, in your future.
Keep being positive, always with a smile, keep the

hope. The contrary will move you away from your destiny. Do not fall for the trap of being negative or to simply conform to what life puts in your way. Focus on victory, success, and be an enthusiast. A person who knows about enthusiasm will never develop it in another, but a person who is an enthusiast will soon have enthusiastic followers.

The salesman who is an enthusiast does not need to ever worry about having enthusiastic followers. In the same way, a teacher who is an enthusiast does not worry about its students being disinterested. Enthusiasm is contagious; it makes things to be looked in a positive light. The results come in proportion to the enthusiasm applied. Enthusiasm is simple, "This is big." Here is the why.

An example of enthusiasm at its maximum can be seen in the walk organized by a famous comedian in Puerto Rico to benefit the Oncology Hospital in the capital, San Juan, Puerto Rico. He achieves that thousands of people follow him and has received thousands of dollars in donation for the noble cause. We can compare that event with others that also help charitable institutions that get less results and the difference is made by the ENTHUSIASM that he generates. People follow the individual that believes in what he is saying. Give life to what you speak.

There is a notable doctor, speaker and writer that makes the following questions: Are your 'good mornings' really good? Does your 'how are you?' show real interest? When you make a habit of

coloring your words with sincere feelings, you
will note a great ascent in your capacity for
holding attention.

Put life in everything you do. Enthusiasm, or the lack
of it, manifest through anything you say or do. When
shaking hands, really shake them. Make your hand
shaking send the message: "I'm happy to meet you,"
and "I am happy to see you again." A
cautious handshake is worse than nothing.
You can notice that fortunate people greet others
with vitality. Make sure your "Thanks" mean
"Thanks, thanks a lot."

***"We have everything we need to be happy. We
simply don't have the correct perspective or we don't
realize it."***

"Vision without action is just a dream. Action without vision just passes the time. Vision with action can change the world."

Jack Welch

VISION WITH ACTION

Studies tell us that we move forward towards what we see regularly. You should keep something in front of you, even if it is symbolic, to remind yourself of what is in your goal, that thing you want to achieve to make your dream true.

When I was a little boy, I would observe that my father had on top of a table various models of houses. Not long after, those four models became what today is Urbanización Villas del Caribe in Santa Isabel,

Puerto Rico. Each time he saw his models he
became closer to his dream until it became a reality.
For a person with limited economic resources
and a manager of social services profession,
recreating the dream of building a suburb in
which 74 families could have their houses, makes
it an extraordinary deed. With the passing of
time I understood that vision with the correct action
has the correct results.

As I started working in one of the best insurance
companies I had the opportunity of chatting with an
industrial psychologist about how to maintain that
vision in front of us. A coworker, José and I,
who started on the same day at the company, were
very attentive to the talk especially when it
was mentioned we should have a picture of

something material we wanted to get as a product of our wok so that "each time we'd look at the picture we would be closer to getting it." The next day José arrived with his photo, a beautiful two-story house on a hill in Coamo. I already had a new house, so I arrived with a picture of a latest model Volvo Turbo 240 which I used to call "the machete of work". After 18 months José was building he house of his dreams and I was driving my Volvo producing insurance policies daily. It also took us to winning awards at the first sales convention. From then on I understood and have made it a part of my life.

If you think you are not reaching your maximum potential, not because you lack faith, talent or determination, but because you are not keeping the correct things in front of you. You should have all over the house pictures and paintings that inspire you, Bible verses that encourage you and mementos that strengthen your faith. Maybe you can have an extra key in your keychain, and if someone asks you can say it is for the new house you will have. Remember to keep that picture in your bathroom mirror, work briefcase or desk. Let that seed reach your interior. I recommend that you look at it and say out loud "Thank you God because you make my dream come true. Thanks, because I will become everything that you created me for." Surely God will increase the size of your vision.

Many studies confirm that the mind thinks with images, not with words, and if we visualize in our minds what we want, it will become a reality.

The power of visualization can be seen often in sports. Athletes review the test or events in their minds many times before it happens. They concentrate completely in a positive result. If we could talk frankly with Olympic events winners we could convince ourselves that each one of them visualized the race as an event they won and arriving to the podium they visualized. This is just one example of drawing upon positive imagination to create images that will take us to success. The more precise those images are and you feel them with more intensity, you will have higher probabilities of obtaining the desired result. Remembering always that the vision must be accompanied by the action to produce that positive result.

MENTAL ATTITUDE AND SALES

Each sale starts in the salesman's mind. Before you
can sell something to someone first you have to be
convinced yourself that you will achieve that sale. If
you do not believe in yourself, in your company
or in your product, is less probable you can convince
others of the contrary.

Some of my best moments during the first stages
of my career as a salesman were when I was
surrounded by a group of very experienced
and successful sales professionals. I loved listening
to them exchanging stories about their biggest and
most spectacular sales. One of them told about how

he knocked on the door of a particular hard to

approach potential client, how another one

closed the sale that seemed impossible to obtain .

and how someone had a picky client who became

the best references source for potential clients,

something he never would have thought possible. The

stories were told one after the other.

Not only did I find these stories fascinating, but

also, I learned a lot from them about the art

of selling. One of the things that Fernando, one

of the group leaders, mentioned and that I

always remember is that to become the winner you

were created to be, you need courage because the

winner runs the race in the way he wants to run it.

The runner has to accept the fact that he can't

make everyone happy, can't be liked by everyone

and will never win over all his critics. Even if you change and do everything others asked of you there will be some that will still find faults. We spend too much time trying to impress people, trying to win their approval, asking ourselves what they will think if we accept the job in sales insurance, if we're wearing new clothes or if we move to a different house.

Instead of running our race, frequently we make decisions far from being loyal to our own person. Experience tells us that in sales the harder closings are within the family and close friends' circles. Not until they see you with "success" will they start recommending you. That is why is necessary to run out and start making sales to new faces, you will see how good it will go. During years in the insurance industry I could observe,

particularly in the life insurance and health

supplementary, that those are offered in many

occasions by agents in pairs. This means that two

agents go out to work and offer the product together.

It is nothing bad by itself, but you have to observe

who is accompanying you. You should be

especially attentive towards people that need

high maintenance. Those kinds of people are

almost impossible to please. They need to be called in

their own timetable, keep them happy, leave them

notes and comply with their demands. If you do not

they get mad, disappointed and will do anything to

make others feel guilty. High maintenance people

tend to be in a majority controlling people too.

If you are not careful they will make you fit in their

mold. They are not interested in you, but in what you

can do for them. Their time is too valuable to

worry about others or make them happy. I know

people who spend more time worrying

about what others think of them than in their own

dreams and goals. You must be free of that. The sales

career requires goals so that when you reach them they

produce the desired well-being. If you want to make

something big out of life, if you want to be a great

salesman, a great business person, a great father or

mother, and a winner, not everyone will cheer you on.

I would love to tell you that all your family, friends

and coworkers will celebrate you, but sadly that

is not the case.

Some will not be capable of deal with the success you

have. If you stay where you were 10 years ago, they

will have no problem with you. But once you start

having success, when God spreads his favor,

some will be jealous and will find faults, it will

pass by like water through the fingers. Your destiny

is too big to get distracted, always remembering

that your decision of success is more important

than anything.

"The key to success depends only of what we can

do in the best way possible."

H.W. Longfellow

Success means many marvelous and positive things.

Success means personal prosperity, an appealing home,

vacations, travels, new things, financial security, giving

your children the most advantages. Success means

gaining admiration, leadership, being viewed with

respect, being free of worries, fears, frustrations and

failures. Success means self-respect, continuously

finding more satisfaction and happiness in life, the possibility of doing more for the people that depend on you. Success means triumph. Success or realization is the goal of life.

BELIEVE YOU CAN HAVE SUCCESS AND YOU WILL

Through the years and the practice of commercial property insurance agent I have had the opportunity to connect with many entrepreneurs. As we all know, some fail in risky business, not everyone has success. However, when I talked to the ones that failed is common to listen to a big number of reasons and excuses for that failure. These are some excuses heard on those conversations: "Truthfully, I never thought that would work" or "I had my doubts even before starting" or "It does not surprise me it did not give any result." The attitude of 'ok, we will try but I do not think it will work' produces failures. The lack of beliefs is a negative power. When the mind does not believe or doubts, attracts 'reasons' to support the failure. Doubt, incredulity, subconscious will to fail, not really wishing for success are the thoughts responsible for the majority of failures. Think of doubt and you will fail, think of victory and you will have success.

Believing is the thermostat that regulates what we achieve in life. Observe the coworker that drags his feet in mediocrity. He thinks his value is small, so he receives little. Believes he cannot do big things and does not do them. Believes he is not important, so anything he does has a "non-important" tag. As times goes by the lack of belief in yourself is demonstrated in words, movements and acts. Unless you change or readjust that thermostat

in a positive belief you will go on becoming smaller
 in your own estimation and before the people that
surround you.

On the other hand, if we examine the path of the
person who is moving forward and believes his value
is big, he will receive a lot. Believes he can manage big
and difficult things and he does. Anything he
does; the way in which he governs himself with
other people, his character, thoughts and points of
view, everything tells us "Here is a professional."
That is an important person.

We are a product of our own thoughts. Adjust your
personal thermostat forward. Manifest your success
with an honest and sincere belief that you can
succeed. Look at the sales convention, the prizes,

and the recognition of your company and your coworkers as an additional motivation for yours and your family's wellbeing. Surround yourself in the power of the belief. Believe in yourself and the good things will happen. Your mind is a "thoughts factory," a hard working factory that produces innumerable thoughts a day. Your thoughts factory production is in charge of two helpers; one of them we can call it "Mr. Success" and the other "Mr. Failure." Mr. Success is in charge of producing positive thoughts. His specialty is producing reasons for which you can, you are qualified, you want and you will. The other helper, Mr. Failure, produces negatives and despicable thoughts. He is an expert in developing reasons for which you cannot, you are weak, you are inadequate, and you are not prepared. His specialty is the chain of thoughts "for which you will fail."

The two helpers are extremely obedient and they will respond to what you order them. All you need to do to signal each helper (success or failure) is give the simple mental disposition. If the signal is positive, Mr. Success will move forward and start working. At the same time, a negative signal will make Mr. Failure show up. Let us show an example of how these two helpers work. Starting the day, tell yourself: "Today is a problematic day." To this signal Mr. Failure enters and creates some facts in demonstration that you are right. The suggestion that it is too hot, that business will be bad during the day, that there will be no sales, another agent is surpassing you, the boss is in a bad mood, and so on, Mr. Failure is very terribly efficient. In a matter of minutes you will be convinced that it is a disastrous day, it deceived you. Before you know it you'll be tangled up in negative thoughts and similar day. If on the contrary, you say "Today is a magnificent day," Mr. Success will be called to act forward; it will obey extremely fast and will tell you "This is a marvelous day." The temperature is refreshing, excellent day to make business, it will be a great day for sales and services. It will be a good day.

And so on, Mr. Failure will be able to show why you cannot sell and it will convince you that you will not succeed, and Mr. Success will convince you of the opposite demonstrating why you can sell or why the customer must buy. It will depend on how much work we will give to each one of our helpers. If Mr. Failure is given more work to do, he will take more space in your mind. It will definitely take charge of producing thoughts of the negative nature. Certainly, there's something to do and its fire Mr. Failure. You do

not need it, do not want to have him by you side

saying you cannot, will fail or things like that.

Mr. Failure cannot help you to get where you

want to be, so put him on the street. Make use of

Mr. Success (100%) a hundred per cent of your

time. When any thought enters your mind, ask

Mr. Success to go work for you. He will show you

how you can have success.

MOVE FORWARD

Once you start the practice of choosing the positive thought it will lead to a conduct of avoiding damaging people. Sadly, there are some people who see the world as a big problem and in their eyes you are a part of it. You know this type of individuals, it does not matter how good things are, they concentrate in the small negative details and they always do. Is a habit that completely destroys relationships: a load of negative energy. These persons are harmful to the health, I advise to keep them away from your surroundings.

I know you must be thinking "but my friend isn't like that" or "my coworker in the office isn't like that."

Does this mean you should turn your back each
time someone tells you of his or her problems?
The answer is NO. Go the farther away possible and
the fastest you can. Run! Constant negativity will end
up absorbing the life that is in you. We are not talking
about someone who has a genuine problem, and
that really needs help. When we refer to harmful, is
to people who are always complaining, who feel
pleasure in finding the bad little piece, the defect,
and see everything as garbage. Usually they are
very cynical, always talking about why you cannot do
this or that, especially about ideas. Their most
important moment of the day is to squash a positive
idea. Do not have contact with these people.
Remember is always your choice. If doing it implicates
a separation from some persons, well you will
overcome it, move forward.

EXCUSES, FAILURE'S ILLNESS

Cure yourself from the "excusitis." Each failure keeps this illness in its advanced form and the majority of people have at least one bout of her.

If we observe that "excusitis" explains the difference between the people who are reaching their goals and the person who succinctly maintains his own situation, we can see with a detailed observation of people that the more fortunate the individual is the less inclined he or she is to offer up excuses. Let us make the effort to not use excuses, eliminate explanations; what does not have, it does not do, because you cannot and because they are not.

I have never met, or have not heard or

read about any person highly accomplished in sales,

or a great business person or leader in their

field, who even when he could have used any

kind of excuse; for example, Roosevelt not being

able to movie his legs, Truman's lack of a

college education or Mary Kay Ash not having a car to

drive to her first sales job, they all left their limitations

behind to achieve success. We should pay special

attention to three things that can help us cure the

intelligence excuses:

1. Never underestimate your own intelligence and

    never overestimate other people's intelligence.

    Do not self yourself at low price, concentrate on

    your advantages. Discover your superior talents,

    remember is not how much brains you have,

but most important how you use your brain, that is what counts. Manage your wishes instead of worrying about the achieved quotient.

2. Reconsider a few times a day, "my attitudes are more important than my intelligence." At work and at home practice a positive attitude. See the reasons why you can do it, not the reasons why you cannot. Use them to win.

3. Remember that the capacity of thinking is of much more value than the capacity of remembering facts. Am I using my mental capacity to make history or am I suing it to remember the history others made?

On occasions we have heard people of all ages use the excuse of age. "I can't do what I want or my age incapacitates me. I am too old or too young to do that or work in that."

One time I interviewed a friend, Nelson, and I offered him a position in sales. Imagine what the answer he gave was. "I'm too old for a sales insurance career. I'm 42 years old." We talked a bit about it and I found the medicine for what he thought was his problem of being too old. All that philosophy of "you are the age you feel you have" did not work with him. But suddenly I asked him: "Nelson, when does a man's productive life begins?" He looked up, meditated for a few seconds and said: "When he's around 22 years old, I guess." Ok, then I told him: "Now, when does a man's productive life end?". "Well," he said,

"if he stays in good shape, healthy and likes his job,

he should be useful until 72 years old."

  Perfectly I added, "a big quantity of individuals

are highly productive after reaching 72 years,

let me convert what you just said. The productive

years of a man nowadays encompass from 22 years

of age until 72 years of age. This is an interval of 50

years or half a century." Nelson listened as I kept

saying; "you're 42 years old now. How many years

of your productive ones have you used up?" "20,"

he answered. "How many are still left?"

His reply: "30."

  Nelson had only depleted 40% of his productive life.

In other terms, he had not even reached the middle

point of his productive time. He has 60% of what you know to be productive time. He has to keep working. I think that after this conversation Nelson cured himself of the age excuse. It is up to him, and to all of us, to avoid these excuses. Nelson connected his thought to "I'm still young." He realized that how old we are is not important. It is the attitude towards age what makes it either a blessing or an obstacle. When you defeat the age excuse, the natural result is gaining youth's optimism and feeling young. When we tear down the fears of age limitations you add years to your life as well as success.

I always remember an ex coworker, don Jesús, better known as don Chu. This man started his career as an insurance agent at 60 years old; he was part of a first class salesforce and was the personal business

sales leader for a decade. He was the first salesman

in the company to reach a goal of one million dollars

on insurance in a year. After 12 years of service he

retired at 72. On the occasion of his retire he

mentioned that the 10 most productive years of

his life were those in the sales insurance business

from his 62 to 72 years of age. He taught us to

look at the horizon with enthusiasm is a big part

of success.

SELLING WITH ENTHUSIASM

From my point of view, the basis of enthusiasm in the services sales is in knowing that customers are benefiting from my product or service. When you believe in what you sell with your heart and mind, others are inclined to feel the same way.

I always remember fondly a conversation with a sales agent, in which she told me she had not been successful selling the cancer cover policies at a public school. I asked her: What factor do you consider makes them not interested in your product? She replied: When I mention I have a great cancer cover policy they instantly answer they already have one and are not interested in changing it. She was disarmed and did not know how to respond, only saying thanks and leaving. I listened to her and recommended she changed her introduction because it will keep happening if she did not. She asked what she could do and I recommended she do what another successful insurance agent, Paul, did. He told me the story about when he visited one or more prospects who he suspected of already having insurance, because of their work place or social condition, he started by asking them what health supplementary cover policy they had, any answer they give he then has the information to continue with his sales pitch. I also remember when he said that, once precisely in front of a group of teachers from the Department of Education, two of them stood up and said they had the cancer policy and they were not interested. Immediately he 'took the bull by the horns' and told them he came to present a convalescence policy that he thought all of them needed but few had it. He then captured the attention of the teachers with one of the exclusivity cover offered by the company he represented. In the end, he achieved to be listened to and to sell to all present a cancer policy with all the covers especially the convalescence one.

The big difference was the presentation; he started by another cover included in the policy to capture the attention. This situation teaches one thing and that is that you have to be prepared to get those sales. After applying what we know to have the positive attitude the next step is to know your product in depth and the advantages it has for the people who will acquire.

If we summarize the successful service sales process, we have to say it is: having a 100% positive mind, knowing the product and its advantages, and develop and implement some sales techniques.

IDENTIFYING POTENTIAL PROSPECTS

On many occasions I have been asked to define the

Prospects location, and the only practical answer I can

give is my own experience. When I started my career

as a salesman I made an inventory comparing my

active and my passive, in that time I was very young

and felt overwhelmed by the quantity of my

passive. Apparently, I was lacking all the qualities

of a star salesman. I lacked sales experience

and education, I have never had my voice trained,

and that was my passive. In terms of active, I could

only find one thing in my favor, a firm

determination that was almost an obsession, a

fervent and irresistible desire to become a great

salesman. I considered this an active because I

have never heard of a person having success

without wanting it. However, I knew that if I wanted

to make my desire a reality the first thing I could do

was study and analyze all sales people I knew, and

using that as a beginning point I started formulating

my own plan. I dedicated myself to improve

my voice and my personality, my presentation method,

how to refute objections, and how to make

appointments and sales. That is when I realized what I

as missing, my progress, my studies, the time I

dedicated to improve my talent and abilities was

worth nothing if there weren't a significant number

of prospects to apply them to. A dentist cannot take

out a tooth if he does not have a patient. In other

words, if there were no people I could see I could

not sell. I went back to observe professional

and prosperous salesmen I knew and I asked them

all the same question: After you decided on a career

in sales, which is the most important quality as

salesman to develop? All of them in one way or the

other gave me the same answer: the ability to

find prospects. In other words, see the right persons

at the right moment. In effect, it does not matter much

what you sell; insurance, shares, medical equipment,

cars, kitchen pots, real estate or any other product

or service, your ability to locate prospect will

determine your success. The bigger your prospects list,

and how much you know about those prospects,

the bigger the number will be of qualified prospects

and bigger the average of sales closings. I can tell

you something after more than 30 years of

experience and it is that the answer to the question

I asked the group of successful sales person is

the correct one; you have to develop the ability of

finding prospects.

There are a few methods to successfully finding

prospects. In general terms these different methods

could be classified in six subtitles.

First there are the cold sales. This plan is probably the

least popular among salespeople and the least used. It

consists of visiting persons, total strangers, all day long.

This is not a very productive use of your time, but I

have met people who have used it with some degree

of success.

Second, the observation method. Some salesmen

think this is much more than just looking. The

sales person must keep his eyes and ears open
looking for all opportunities that present
themselves with new people, situations
and circumstances.

Third, the never-ending chain of referrals or
connections. This plan is closer to the ideal method
of finding prospects. As the name says it is when the
salesman starts a chain of referrals. This happens when
each time a sales is closed you ask the customer a name
of someone they think might be interested in the
product, and once you have sold to that one you ask
for more referrals and this continues indefinitely.

Fourth, prior customers. One of the sources that will
give you big transactions is your prior customers. In
many cases they will be friendly, and will show an

interest in cooperating with and helping you. However, many sales people have the habit, strange as it is, of neglecting them, and one day they will discover their old customer has become another's salesman prospect.

Fifth, the nest. A magnificent sales system is making sales or having prospects in the same office or company, this way you build a sales nest all in the same place, business or profession.

Sixth, influential centers. This is a system based on a simple premise. The easiest and most effective way to reach a person is through another one who is appreciated and respected. When you create an association with this type of person you will have a powerful influential center from where you can get an innumerable quantity of potential prospects. It is incredible the amount of sales that can come from a powerful and well respected client's recommendation. This method in particular has an infinite variety to achieve success.

Never forget that prospects are people. You will say that I am underlining something that is so obvious it does not need pointing out but believe me it is not. In any system to select prospects, before you select who can be a prospect or a potential customer you should study all the persons you see. The success you can achieve finding prospects does not depends on any of those people you do not know. You are responsible for your own success and, at the same time, success depends on your attitude and way of thinking. Start internalizing the idea that people are not more than that, people. In reality all of them

are prospects for what you sell. If you internalize
that idea and energetically adopt the right attitude
you will be surprised at how different people are.
Very soon your mental change will produce a more
notable change for a different reaction to what you
once considered to be a crowd.

  If you are a new prospects finder the ideal place
where to start is your home. Ask your husband
or wife or other members of your family to help you.
In first place, make an inventory of prospects,
write down their names, addresses and phone
numbers of all the people you and your family know.
Do not worry if they are interested or not in what
you are selling, you can add that information later
on. Now put all that information in your archive
system database (if electronic better) and add

on additional information such as place of work,

job position, approximated income, and how many

family members there are. This will give you a

clearer idea of the product that you can offer to

that prospect. The important thing about

finding prospects is that you can have a well from

where good names flow constantly. The words

from famous Chinese wise man Confucius "Dig

the well before you thirst" apply here.

It is important to pay attention to the prospects list,

the names of those who because of their

social or economic conditions, or both, are people

who can be considered as an "influential centers."

This can be defined as an important person in

the community or workplace. Generally, they are

leaders who enjoy the respect and admiration from

many people in their circle. These "influential centers" are the ones that once you turned them into customers put you in an important place; they give you standing as a sales professional. Other people such as family members, coworkers, members of the community etc. follow these "influential centers." They too can easily go to your list of prospects and eventually become your customers.

Let us remember that the prospect that is referred by an "influential center" normally respects the person who referred him or her for different reasons that could be intelligence, economic success attained or social status. The important thing is that this type of referral creates a predisposition to acquire the product that was recommended, and it is going to depend on your preparation

and knowledge to finalize the sale and continue

the possible referral chain that could lead you to

another "influential center".

Experienced salespersons have gone through this,

and believe me; people new in sales will go through

it too. You just have to be very awake and attentive

to obtain the maximum benefit from the sales

operation that will surely lead you to your desired

success faster.

If you as a salesman manage to impress your

customer with knowledge and enthusiasm, he or

she will want to help you; ask them for referrals and

you will see that you will have a successful career, it

is a wheel that has already been invented, but please

put it in practice. The more "influential centers" you get, the more sales you can make. You will also notice when you meet with other successful salespeople, that not necessarily the one who works the more hours is the one with the best results. The words "getting up early does not make the sun rise earlier" apply here.

When I started in the sales path as an insurance agent there was a very professional sales group in our office, but as always there are some that stand out and guess what? I observed the number one and number two in sales for a long time. The leader in sales at that time, Fernando, was someone who always looked calm and quiet. He always took time to play golf during the week, or would play softball with the "all timers" on weekends, or participate in the fishing club. In other words, the man had fun while working.

On the other hand, the second in sales, Edwin,

who would exchange the top position with

Fernando, was also a fun, civic person. He was

a member of the Lions Club International, Chamber

of Commerce, Rotary Club, and Caballeros de Colón,

everything you could imagine. He was seen having fun

all the time and the numbers always growing. I learned

that it was not necessarily the hours in the office or

looking for sales what would give me accomplishment,

it was something more. I identified it as the

tremendous force of habits. Good habits can take

us to guarantee the future, prosperity and good

health. But on the other hand, bad habits take

us to failure. The baits one by one can be fragile,

but when they are interconnected like chain links

they gain strength and can mold us as a person.

Good habits like attitude, work enthusiasm, waking up early, planning for finding prospects, time dedicated to find prospects should be more than that of my competitors. Good work habits have to be practiced every day and they will surely lead you to success.

While I was observing these two sales coworkers in the office I noticed they both had excellent habits in the job. Both were very organized, practiced the thirst for sales constantly, that is why they had "dug the well" before being thirsty, as Confucius said. They had something very important I identify as "sense of opportunity." Both were great time synchronizers, when to talk about business or about their insurance product, when to share time with potential customers. This sense of opportunity must be put to action with the precision a surgeon uses to make an incision in order for it to bring good results.

I am referring to when you spend time with potential customers you should, after identifying them, qualify them, and then with a lot of empathy (which means putting yourself in the place of the other) bring the topic of how can we help or benefit them. Through that synchronizing the prospect will understand that he is benefiting from his relationship with you. These two coworkers, Fernando and Edwin, were really extraordinary, they had developed the "sense of opportunity" to make sales. Until this day I had resolved to have one good habit for work and having the "sense of opportunity" always "On" in everything I do.

The great importance of the finding of prospects is that in order to have sales there have to be someone to sell to. How do we find them? Some sources are daily and regionals newspapers, phone books, commerce guide and registries, business magazines, among many others. Sending congratulatory cards to existing customers or potential prospects is always productive. They may be for birthdays, Christmas, or any other particular celebration; they all create a good impression. That is why is advisable that you obtain personal details like phone number, address, email and birth date from all your customers. If you have the good work habit of sending, or having your assistant send, a congratulatory email to someone on their birthday, that person will think of you when you do. I had the welcome experience in various occasions of having customers call me to say thanks for the greetings I sent them

around Christmas or their birthdays. Sometimes

they mentioned that I was the only person

who remembered that detail, even when many of

them were successful business people or professionals

they did not receive any other message. Believe me

that this will put you on the favorites list and you

will make sales for a long time, generally, these

persons become "influential centers" or a referrals

source.

Time is important, always take into consideration

that the time you use today in finding prospects will

produce tomorrow's sales. The sales process

encloses motivation for the customer or prospect

and to the salesman. It is necessary that the salesman

motivates himself, must practice it constantly

because if he or she is not motivated to achieve the

sales it won't be able to convey the necessary

enthusiasm so the buyer gets motivated to buy.

NOBODY SAID IT WAS EASY

The sales career is not easy, requires a lot of dedication. The statistics from the Department of Labor of the United States are proof of it. They reflected some important facts; from the work population in the United States an 84% can correctly work on a project as long as it has been planned and the personnel has constant supervision, 14% can follow up with a plan without supervision, but only 2% is able to take on a project and bring it to its happy conclusion without direction or any assistance of any type. The sales profession is in that exclusive and auto-motivated 2%. It should not surprise us that the modern salesman who has self-confidence is proud of his work or constantly fights to better his or her abilities and interior motivation.

For the sake of keeping in shape I invite you to review and examine some motivation points that follow. These pursue professional improvement.

1.   Enthusiasm and organized activity always go hand in hand.

2.   Honesty generates trust and trust is the basis of all the sales you make.

3.   Courtesy. A courteous person always is treated with courtesy and creates a very nice atmosphere.

4.   Initiative is the best salesperson's active, with this you control your own destiny.

5.   Constancy is the force that never gives up and is one of the professional sales person's personality traits.

6.   Action. This is the most important motivational point, only with action can you transform ideas, plans, and wished in realities. Action starts with your prospects archive, keeping it updated with a correct qualification of each name in each card.

Take the test. Examine yourself in all these motivational points, do it every morning for a week before you go out to work and observe if your task of finding prospects improves. Success in locating prospects does not require a special type of genius but it does require constancy and perseverance.

.

OBJECTIONS IN THE SALES PROCESS

Nobody has said the sales profession is easy so it is very difficult that someone who has no talent can get behind it.

The successful salesperson tends to develop an attitude of service. To achieve it, there are some elements required like having a high esteem for your job and yourself. Prepare like a good lawyer or doctor dedicates time to education and training. You do not have to become a psychologist, but knowing something of people's social psychology will help a lot, especially when during a presentation you encounter objections.

The professional salesman who is sure of himself and the basis of that assuredness is, in great measure due to the knowledge of the product and the benefits it can offer, will bless that objection when it arrives. The first thing said is "Thank God for that objection," as prepared as a salesperson is he will never be complete, however, the objection will allow to explain in details the benefits the product offers or the losses it could help avoid.

ATTITUDE AGAINST OBJECTIONS

The objections are not many, and usually they get repeated. The most important thing to do in the face of objections is to listen attentively to it. The worse one is a resounding NO. With objections you can demonstrate that you listen carefully. Quickly pass judgement about the attitude that is presented with that objection, if what the prospect wants to show is security, prestige, self-image, or that he is the audience leader. There are times that it is not what the prospect says but how it is said. The best is to let him/her speak, listening and letting them know with your body language, without interrupting, that what is being said it is interesting. The prospect will give you valuable information on how to sell to him/her, very probably giving the conditions under which to buy your product. In that moment after you have listened follow up by making a flattering comment because if you contradict the person it will be like throwing wood to the fire and you will not achieve the sale which is the goal. Make a conciliatory statement, not that you are in agreement with the prospect's position, is about showing that you understand and have empathy. This is a technique, is we want to call it that way, which you have to practice until you can master it very naturally.

Treat that objection as a question so you can answer it, at the same time, posing a question about the objection's content will give the one who made the objection to answer his own doubt or questioning. Once you have answered it, forget it and continue with your presentation. Remember it's practice. There is a moment I experienced that, although it does not have anything to do with sales, made an impact in me. Once I spent time with a great baseball player, today part of the Big Leagues Hall of Fame, during a game in New York City. I asked him if all players arrived so early to each game's practice like he did, and he replied that he did it because if during the defense practice he missed catching one ball, he would ask for 100 consecutive balls by the same side until he did not miss any. To me, this is a clear attitude that you have to pay the price. This practice took him to become a member of the Hall of Fame.

Definitely, practice and preparation before making a sales presentation will surely make the closings average of a winner.

THE IMPORTANCE OF HAVING GOALS

First, what is the definition of goal? If you do not have it clear you can lose the path before starting. We have heard many answers through the years, I like one in particular.

A goal is the constant pursue of a valuable objective until it is reached"

I invite you to reflect on the words that make up this statement. "Constant" means that is a process that takes time. "Pursue" indicates that you are following something; there is a probability of obstacles and barriers to overcome. "Valuable" demonstrates that the pursuing is worth it, that after the difficult times there is a big reward at the end. "Until it is reached" expresses that you will whatever's necessary to complete the process. It is not always easy but of great importance if you want a life filled with extraordinary achievements. This is what really should motivate you to the final result of achieving the goal.

Following is a list to verify if you are doing the correct thing to establish your goals.

1. You must establish the most important goals yourself. This sounds obvious; however, a common mistake is allowing others to establish the principal goals. Maybe it is being done by the company you work for, the industry you are a part of, your Friends or even the neighbors. The question that must be asked is: What do I really want to do? When you let another person or group of people define what success is, you are sabotaging your own future. Do not allow it. Even the media has one of the biggest influences over us in respect to making decisions and the majority of people fall into it every day. Media defines success related to the clothes we wear, the cars we drive, houses we live in, and the vacations we take. Depending on how much we adjust into these categories it is determined if you are a failure or a success. The important thing is that you decide to give your own definition to success and stop worrying about what the rest of the world thinks. For years, the founder of one of the most successful clothes store chains in history, used to enjoy driving an old Ford truck, even though

he was one of the richest men in the United States.
Once he was asked why he did not drive a car
that showed more his position and he answered:
"Well, I like my truck." So, forget about image and
establish goals that are adequate for you. But if you
want to drive a luxurious car, live in a beautiful house,
or have an exciting lifestyle, work for it! Just be
sure it is something you want and that you are doing
it for the right reasons.

2. **Goals must be important**. Before writing down
future goals, ask yourself: What is important to me?
What is the objective of doing this? What am I
prepared to give up for this to happen? Thinking
this way will increase clarity. Is very important you
do so. The reasons to start a new course of action
are what drives you and fill you with energy to wake

up in the morning, even on days you do not want

to. Ask, what are the rewards and benefits in

acquiring a new discipline? Concentrate on

the new and exciting lifestyle that you can enjoy if you

compromise to act now. If this really does not activate

your adrenaline, look at the other side of the coin. If

you keep on doing the same thing always, how will

your lifestyle be in five years, in 10 or 20 years? How

can you describe your financial future if you

do not commit to changes? What about your health,

your relationships and the quantity of free time you

have to share with family and friends? Will you

enjoy much more freedom or will keep on working

many more hours a week? Avoid saying "would have."

As a great philosophy master said, discipline weights

pounds, but regret weights tons when you let

life pass through without accomplishments.

In some years you won't want to see the past and say: "If I would have taken that opportunity, if I would have saved and invested with regularity, if I would have spent more time with my family, if I would have stopped visiting the casino, if I would have taken care of my health." Remember, it is your decision. Lastly, you are responsible of every decision you make, so choose wisely. Commit now to establishing goals that guarantee future freedom and success.

3. **Remember that goals must be specific and quantifiable.** Most people get lost on this point. This is one of the reasons people never achieve what they are capable of. They never define what they want with precision. Vague generalizations and fast statements are not enough. For example, if you say: "My goal is to be more independent economically speaking," what does that mean? For some people economic independence is having two million dollars saved and invested, for others is making $100 thousand a year or simply not having debt. What is it for you? What is your number? If this is an important goal for you, devote time to find out. Whichever the goal is must be written down and the key is to be specific, challenge yourself with words. Repeat it until the goal is clear and quantifiable. By doing so it will increase the possibilities of achieving the desired results. A common example at the start of a new year is many people say: "I'm going to start exercising," but this is a very general definition, there is no way to measure it. When specifically you say: "I'm going to exercise 30 minutes daily, four days a week, Monday, Wednesday, Friday and Saturday from 7:00 am to 7:30 am. 20 minutes on a treadmill,

10 minutes of weights and in a month it will change
to 30 minutes on the treadmill and 20 minutes on
weights". That is a specific and quantifiable goal; it
will be possible to measure progress. After all, a goal
without a number is not more than a motto.

4. **Goals must be flexible.** A flexible plan offers
enough freedom to change plans if an opportunity
presents itself that you cannot and should not waste.
In the prior example the exercise hours could get
changed for schedule reasons or because something
unplanned comes up, but it must be done if we want
to reach the goal.

5. **Goals must be exciting and represent
a challenge.** It does not matter what your goal is,
write it down. Does not matter how ridiculous it

may look, do not judge it at that moment. It was after many years that I realized that things I achieved for example during my childhood were goals that were very defined in an occasion. As an adult, I could observe that the little book I took to church for catechism class had a note on the back cover that said "I am going to be an altar boy on the town's principal church after I graduate catechism." That goal became a reality with mathematician accuracy just as I wrote it down at 12 years old. It was exciting for me and it represented a challenge because there were other altar boys already and no one had told me they were looking for one, and there were many other interested boys. We have to remember that what can be exciting for one person does not have to be for another. Remember to write it down and only share it with other persons who can help you achieve it.

When you establish exciting and challenging goals it generates an encouragement that prevents falling into a boring life. To achieve it you must get out of what is comfort for you. Maybe you do not have to have as big challenges as the explorer Goddard's of going to the North and South Pole and sail around the globe (he did it in four occasions),but get away from mediocrity, think big. Establish goals that excite you so much that you can barely fall asleep. Life has a lot to offer, Why not enjoy what you deserve?

6. Goals must be in accordance with your values. Synergy and flow are two words that define any process that advances towards its completion without effort. When your goals are in line with your fundamental values the mechanism to achieve harmony is put in movement. Which are your fundamental values? Anything that makes you feel secure and that vibrates in the most profound fibers of your being. They are the fundamental beliefs, those you have grown up with and have molded your character; honesty and integrity for example. When you take advantage of the fundamental values you have in order to achieve positive, exciting and important goals, the decision making becomes easy. The key is to remember and put into work the positive attitude. If you keep your mind filled with the correct thought, there will not be space for incorrect thoughts. You must be focused at all times in the positive and you will notice that each day will be productive. Keep the correct people that will help you achieve your goals and at the same time theirs.

7. Goals must be balanced. It is interesting, if you

had to live again, what would you do differently? When this question is asked to 80 years old people, they never say "I'd spend more time in the office" or "Would've used more time looking for business." No, instead they clearly reply they would travel more, spend more time with family and have more fun. Then, when you establish goals make sure to include areas that allow for time to relax and enjoy the best things in life.

8. Goals must be based in reality; "be a realist."

It is correct that we have to think big. However, thinking realistically will ensure that results will be better. It is important being realistic when setting t he time frame it will take you to achieve the goal. An example of this: if you earn $36 thousand a year and your goal is to be a millionaire in three months, that is not realistic. As a general rule, for new companies usually you will duplicate the time you think will take to start. Generally, legal obstacles will emerge, government regulations, financial challenges, etc. that initially hold you back. They must be taken on with intelligence and verticality. The important thing is not to set goals that are pure fantasies. If you were five feet tall, maybe you will never be the central blocker of the volleyball national team. So, whatever happens think positively and big and try to have an exciting view of the future, make sure the plan is a real one and that you gave it a reasonable time to make it happen.

"If your heart is set in what you want, there will be nothing that can be done to prevent you from obtaining it."
Andrew Carnegie

9. Going back to the basics. Remember to always learn from those who have made it. As I mentioned earlier about the famous explorer and adventurer, Goddard is an example of one of the persons who better mastered the process of setting goals. He achieved more in his life than what 100 persons would have done together. On one occasion he was asked how he overcame obstacles and he answered: "When I feel trapped, I start again concentrating in one goal that I can achieve in the next seven days, something simple, I do not think in anything else, which generally after achieving it, gives me a new impulse."

Experts from a behavior study have observed that:

3% of persons have defined goals

10% imagine their goals but do not write them down

60% of people have vague goals

27% have never thought of their future

I invite you to identify which segment you are and to choose to improve. Make the habit of defining your goals. Having goals is the 75% of what you have achieved. Use goals that help you grow. Every right guess in human progress; small or big inventions, medical or scientific discoveries and engineering discoveries were visualized before becoming realities. A goal is an objective, a purpose, is more than a dream, is a dream to act upon, it is clear, and is what we are working towards. Nothing happens, not a step is taken until you have established a goal. Without goals individuals are limited to travel or glide through life, never knowing where they are going and never arriving anywhere. Goals are as

essentials to success as air is to life. Nobody stumbles
with success without a goal. Nobody lives without
air. "The important thing is not where you were
or are, but where you want to be."

All of us have wishes; all of us dream about what we
really want to be, but few give the most for that wish,
on the contrary, we cancel it. I consider there are
four weapons we use to kill success. These must
be destroyed because they could be harmful.

Self-depreciation – How many times have we Heard
people say "I'd like to be a doctor, a lawyer, account
executive, have my own business, be a successful
insurance agent but I can't do it because I lack
intelligence, don't have the education or will fail if I try
it." In the end, many young people destroy their wish

with the old negative of self-depreciation.

1. **Security** – People that say, "I have reached security where I am" (secure employment) use the security weapon to kill their dreams.

2. **Competition** – "The career or field is saturated There are too many people in that field." This is an observation that quickly ruins the wish.

3. **Family** – The attitude of "I should've started five years ago, but now I have a family and can't change." This is a deadly weapon against wishes or goals.

Get rid of these weapons, they are not true. Remember that the developing your complete strength, do what you want to do, is worth it. Surrender to the wish and gain energy, enthusiasm, mental vitality and even better health. It is never too late for the wish to take direction.

TIME IS IMPORTANT

How many times have we heard that time is money, but we do not put it in practice? To maximize production is necessary to plan. That is the basis for every organization. Some essential elements to manage your time are:

1. Define your goal or be specific. Remember that big goals and small goals are equally important.

2. Prepare your program step by step, assign the time each step will take and practice your presentation.

3. You can only do one job at a time. Write it down.

4. How much is the value of your time? Is it all that I do worth the money I perceive? Do not waste your time doing work that others can do for less value. The example I have is the one about a good sales agent that when it was time to change the oil in his car, he skipped work to do it because he knew how to do it, and spent the day doing it. He generated a little more than $250.00 average of daily gain. If you subtract the $35.00 cost of the oil change that is done in about 30 minutes in an authorized dealer, you can get the maintenance done and avoid not gaining $215.00 approximately and wasting your time. Time for finding prospects is important. Value it.

5. Try to avoid routine, learn to delegate so you can increase your work's capacity.

6. Differentiate what is "urgent," what needs to be done today, from what is "important," and maybe can be done the next day.

THE STEP BY STEP METHOD

The step by step method is the only intelligent

resource to reach an objective. A friend who

was successful in the sales field of supplementary

health insurance plans used to say he made it

simple, setting a daily goal, achieving it would get

to complete the weekly goal, which then would lead

to make the monthly goal. This would definitely

take him to achieve the yearly goal set. Adjustments

are made in the daily goal, if it is not reached then the

next day you go out with enthusiasm and without rest

to make the reach the goals of two days. I always

trusted the question: Will this help me to go where

I want to? If the answer is no, leave it, if on the contrary the answer is yes, quickly go ahead. Keep in mind we do not have to do a big thing to jump to success; we will go step by step. We can observe some guides that could help us be more effective, for example:

A. Get rid of these habits

1. Postpone things

2. Use of negative language

3. Talking without action

B. Acquire these habits

1. Do a morning test of your appearance.

2. Plan the night before each day's work.

3. Find prospects among people at the adequate opportunity.

C. Value family and friends

1. Show more appreciation for the small things my partner does.

2. Dedicate at least a daily hour to exclusive attention to my family

3. Make four new friends

D. Sharpen the mind

1.Invert at least two hours each week to read trade and professional magazines. You tube offers excellent sales conferences. It is recommended downloading the application on your cell phone and watch these when you have time to do it.

2. Read self-help books

3. Have serene thoughts at least for half
an hour

When you see a person particularly well centered,
balanced, and with clear thoughts, keep in mind that
person was not born that way. An investment in a big
effort day by day makes the person what it is. Build on
positive new habits and destroying the negative ones
is a daily process.

THE POWER OF INFORMATION

Nowadays, more than ever, because of the great

amount of information available through different

social media and the rapidness which it travels,

is important to pay attention to the negotiation power

of customers.

When customers are concentrated, are many or buy

in bulk, their power of negotiation represents an

important force that affects the intensity of

competition in an industry. If the power of

negotiation is strong, companies may try to change

their offers, on either their product, warranty or

specialty services to get their loyalty.

This information must be also accessed by the sales professionals to improve their knowledge of competitor's offers and to get a better understanding of the products in the market that in one way or another could affect our sales operation.

Information's availability about products and services offer a bigger power of negotiation to customers when:

a.   They can change to other brands or substitute products without excessive costs.

b.   They are especially important to the sales professional.

c.   It is their decision buying a product and when to do it.

d.   They are informed about products, prices and costs of sellers.

e. Sales professionals are fighting against the drop in customer's demand.

As I have said before, the existence of many web places to get information forces companies, sales teams and professionals who offer their services to be very aware of the market's offer and demand, and this forces us to be the best we can be.

A PRAYER

Oh God, creator of all things, help me!

Today I will go out with the disposition to serve those

like me, and I need you to guide me,

without you I will walk away from

the path that leads to triumph and happiness.

Give me challenging tasks but guide me to find in them

the seeds of success.

Strengthen my spirit to be able to face my fears and

give me the courage to

overcome them and laugh about them.

Lord, oh Lord, help this humble salesman.

Amen

THE SALESMAN

AUTHOR'S INFORMATION

➢ Born in New York, New York, Live in Puerto Rico

➢ Graduated with a Bachelor's degree in Business Administration from Universidad Interamericana de Puerto Rico

➢ Graduated with a "Juris Doctor" from Law School of Pontificia Universidad Católica de Puerto Rico

➢ Certified as a Mediator and Neutral Evaluator by the Negociado de Métodos Alternos para la Solución de Conflictos (Alternative Methods for Conflicto Solution Bureau) of the Supreme Court of Puerto Rico

➢ Certified as Arbitrator by the Colegio Universitario de Mediación Profesional (Professional Mediation) and the Negociado de Métodos Alternos para la Solución de Conflictos (Alternative Methods for Conflicts Solution Bureau) of the Supreme Court of Puerto Rico

➢ Principal and Founder of Moreno Cintrón & Asociados, Inc., Firm. Insurance and Bonds

ENEH Management, LLC

PO BOX 7212

Ponce, PR 00732-7212

Email: eneh.management@gmail.com